36.68
YBP

50998

Winner of the L. E. Phillabaum Poetry Award for 2006

Henry Taylor

Crooked
POEMS Run

Louisiana State University Press

Baton Rouge

Published by Louisiana State University Press
Manufactured in the United States of America
First Printing

Designer: Laura Roubique Gleason
Typeface: Centaur
Printer and binder: Edwards Brothers, Inc.

Library of Congress Cataloging-in-Publication Data

Taylor, Henry, 1942–
    Crooked run : poems / Henry Taylor.
        p.   cm.
    ISBN 0-8071-3124-5 (alk. paper) — ISBN 0-8071-3125-3 (pbk. : alk. paper)
    I. Title.
PS3570.A93C76 2006
811'.54—dc22

                                                2005016553

Grateful acknowledgment is made to the editors of the following journals, in which
the poems first appeared, occasionally in somewhat different versions: *American Scholar:*
"A Brief Partnership"; *Antioch Review:* "My Dear Sister Hannah"; *Atlantic Monthly:* "A
Crosstown Breeze," "After High Water," and "A Set of Hoofprints"; *Cincinnati Review:*
"One Way to Go About It"; *Folio:* "Here Reynolds Is Laid"; *Friends Journal:* "Snap-
shots"; *Georgia Review:* "An Artist from Another Place," "Metes and Bounds" and "Boy
Hunting in Bog"; *Iron Horse Literary Review:* "Valentine's Daffodils"; *LandEscapes 2000*
(Washington State University): "Creek Walk (1)"; *Missouri Review:* "Brilliance" and "A
Little Respect"; *Nightsun:* "On the Air"; *Sewanee Review:* "Creek Walk (2)" and "George
Washington's Farewell to His Hounds"; *Shenandoah:* "Summer Hill" and "The Hay-
fork"; *64:* "Hughesville Nights"; *Smartish Pace:* "Aka Fawn Meadow"; *Tar River Review:*
"Stones and Staves"; *Virginia Quarterly Review:* "The Dining Room at Springdale," "A
Straight Stretch on the Far Side of Coolbrook," "A Trace of Old Road Work," and
"Vision at Woods' Edge."

    "My Dear Sister Hannah" is closely based on a letter from Caroline "Car-
rie" Taylor of Purcellville, Virginia, to her sister Hannah Stabler in Sandy Spring,
Maryland. It appears in *Ye Meetg Hous Smal: A Short Account of Friends in Loudoun County,
Virginia, 1732–1980,* by Asa M. Janney and Werner Janney (privately printed, Lincoln,
Virginia, 1980), 45–47.

    For permission to walk stretches of Crooked Run that cross their land, I am
grateful to Mr. and Mrs. Hossein Askari, Jean Brown, Sam and Tim Brown, Ralph
Clark, John Flannery and Bettina Gregory, Dr. and Mrs. James Gable, Kassie Kings-
ley, Anne Ma and David Moyes, Peter Packard, Dr. and Mrs. Joseph M. Rogers, Mr.
and Mrs. James R. Tiffany, and the Reverend and Mrs. Elijah V. White.

For My Mother and
In Memory of My Father

Here is the stream I can't set foot in twice,
however often it has drawn my steps
to thread known rocks and trees toward a place
where the sharp surge of recollection shapes
itself then fades, as brightness fades and drops
groundward when another day's work is done.
Holding to paths engraved on inward maps,
I hunt for ways, as I walk Crooked Run,
to bless these lands, these parents, that I have been their son.

Contents

I

Metes and Bounds

The land surveyor either sets or finds.
You read this in the markings on his plats:
at such-and-such a point a pipe is set,
at older corners planted stones are found.

Still, his is not the boundary that binds.
Wandering through my native hills and flats,
I see what fields are not encompassed yet,
how little time we have to hold our ground.

Creek Walk

In a single hour, between the banks of one small stream,
a heron takes an interrupted walk among crayfish
and frogs, each pause between strides frozen, like a picture,
each stride a slow transition from one stillness to the next.

Without knowing it, maybe, the frog awaits the beak
that strikes so quickly the frame around the picture
stretches out of shape, then snaps back.
The frog goes down the throat, wings lift and settle.

Now, as in ancient times, a beaver slips off the bank
and drops toward a point of buoyancy, his back and face
just out of water, legs moving as in a brisk walk,
the flat tail rowing up and down, leisure in every move.

Then simply gone, not there, as if a strong transparent hand
had lifted him, or shoved him under water—removed him,
anyway, to a place where he must somehow be needed.
Between those two, a sick raccoon is taking his final steps,

as if his illness were a brush-fire he could walk away from,
not rabies, bound to finish him in a day or two at most.
He came here, had his life, and as his last strength goes,
the little branch keeps washing over algae-laden stones.

Snapshots

HENRY B. TAYLOR, 1873–1968

1.

Out of communal silence the people
called Quakers have gathered to themselves
their quiet, steady way of being
in a world they choose not to reject.
In that context my grandfather Taylor thrived.
Presiding Clerk for almost forty years,
he had a gift for finding just the phrase
for rugged matters hard to bring to consensus.
At memorial meetings, especially,
he had a touch that came to be locally famous.
It got to where he was asked to speak
almost every time a Quaker died.
So, inevitably, came the death
of one for whom he had had little use.
An irreverent old rapscallion, he thought,
and tried to stay out of his way.
                                        The man's sons
came back to Goose Creek from distant homes
and found themselves a trifle out of their depth.
Taking advice, they asked Henry B.
to speak. He would have preferred not to,
but didn't see a way to turn them down.
Worked a day or two on a set of remarks
not without justice but sparing the whole truth,
and when the time came, spoke them. Afterwards,
the sons made known their disappointment. "We wanted
an honest-to-God eulogy," they said, and he,
"I'm sorry. You picked two of the wrong men."

2.

His kindly cleanliness of speech,
his upright square dealing, became
community property, almost
proverbial. For his son, an example
awesome, if not impossible.

He set Joe Jackson to work one morning
cleaning off the asparagus patch.
Pretty soon Crave Tate came past,
watched a moment, and observed
that the boss didn't want asparagus
pulled out with the weeds.
It takes years to establish asparagus.
"He said to clean it off," Jackson
replied, "and that's what I'm doin.
Go on bout y'own business.
I know what the man told me."
Tate went on up to the house
seeking clarity and vindication,
and got both, in a voice
that carried across two fields:
"Hell, no!" Not too strong
by some standards, maybe, but
the teenaged boy who would
become my father, in which role
he would think of this moment often,
laughed.
       All but fell down
laughing, in an astonished
seizure of relief
that the old man had it in him,
laughed till he had no more breath for it.

3.

He told me once about a time when silence
was the best response he had to what occurred.
He'd engaged a fellow from out Between the Hills
to caponize some young male chickens
before they could grow up into roosters.
A delicate skill, practiced even then by few.

As he worked along, the fellow mentioned
he'd just that morning been in Hamilton
at the home of Mr. Harrison Branch.
"Mr. Branch a mighty fine man," he said,
"but he's awful quare." Breath held,

a deft small finger-twitch, a chicken set aside.
"They tell me all them Quakers is quare."

4.

"Just look at that old man!" cried Leon Grooms,
and we all did, as he took two quick steps
while looking upward to watch
the steep trajectory of a fresh egg
we had just found in the haymow,
reaching out toward where his shoe tops would be
in another step and a half, letting
the egg fall easily into the soft cradle
he had made of his hands, straightening,
holding it up unbroken, a quick wave
of thanks, then turning back to the weeds
he'd been raking when the wagon passed
down the driveway with us on it, headed back
to the field for another load of hay.
Leon had stood up as we rolled by,
held up our find and called out, "Mr. Taylor,
got an egg for you!" "All right! Throw it here!"
"He mean what he says?" It was an uphill throw
from a moving wagon, not quite thirty yards.
"I never knew him not to," my father said,
and Leon settled back into his windup.

5.

One afternoon he stood with A. M. Janney
on the porch of Janney's Store,
when down the single street came—so quietly!—
a funeral procession, fraught
with somewhat more than the usual pomp.
Asa Moore's stunning voice rang out:
"My goodness, Henry, those people
sure know how to wrap it up, don't they?
Makes our ways look kind of sparse.
Maybe we need a religion
that would take us out like that."
Grandpa said, "What's good enough
to live by is good enough to die by."

6.

At eighty-five, interrupted.
A stroke melted
one side of his face
and stopped him from walking.
Voice thin but speech clear,
he called to me from his wheelchair
as I came into the room,
"Henry, they've got me under!
Yes sir, this time
they've got me under!"
Believing and not believing,
wanting, as always in his presence,
to do right, I made some lame reply.
Yet within months
he was doing a slow dance
with an aluminum walker;
later, two canes, then one.
Went back to gardening.

Nine years later my father
stopped by there on his way home
from an auction, and mentioned
having bought a harness-maker's bench.
"Let's have a look."
So my father brought it in to the porch,
and the old man got up, put a hand
on the two tall wood jaws
of the vise, walked all around the piece,
swung a leg over the seat and sat,
working the vise treadle with his foot.
"Just fine," he said, "just fine."
That night, in his sleep, he died.

7.

When Henry B. Taylor had been dead
for at least twenty years,
I was in Janney's Store myself,
and Asa Moore said, for maybe
the thirtieth time in forty years,

that I could never hope to be
the man my grandfather was.

Correct. But I had come at last
to know I was not called
to be the man another man had been.
Should not have said so.
Asa Moore, I mostly think,
meant well. I mostly wish
I had, too.
           So he was right.

Stones and Staves

Last time I looked, a low circle of stone
still broke through grass at the barn's northeast corner—
the foundation where a wooden silo stood
in the days when my father ran a Guernsey herd.
I watched it being filled a few times,
before he went out of dairying for good
and took the silo down to use the staves.
He lived another forty years or so,
then left me here with questions I still have.

A man named John Hummer, he told me once,
built the silo. A local contractor,
he undertook such work when he was sober.
At other times he made another kind
of name for himself. One night in Purcellville,
at a dance, he got mad at something he figured
had been said or done to him; he went outside
to the parking lot and filled his pockets up
with crabapple-sized stones, got on his horse,
and galloped around the dance hall, throwing rocks
through all the windows, the open and the shut.
Drunk or sober, he had a deadly gift
with a thrown rock; he kept them all surrounded,
hunkered down by the windowsills, until
he cooled off, or ran out of rocks, and rode on home.
After a while that story took on the power
to make people who hadn't been there claim they were.

He came alone to build the silo—no crew,
no scaffolding. Only a ladder. This was odd.
My father watched him set up the bottom tub—
a cylinder of tongue-in-groove staves,
alternating five- and ten-foot lengths.
It had the look of a half-finished basket
if you stood off far enough and saw the air
in six-inch strips between the taller staves,
ready to receive the ten-foot lengths
that would take the job toward the second level.

The tub was held together with iron hoops
about a foot apart, not drawn down tight
until the second stage was put in place.
Most men would build a scaffold for that purpose,
but Hummer used the ladder. He climbed up
and stood on the butt ends of two long staves,
swaying just a little as they flexed,
stooped down and grabbed the end of a fresh one,
heaved it aloft and eased it into a gap.
He rocked it to persuade it; in the last
couple of feet it hung, so down he came
and carried his sledgehammer back up there.
Standing once more on the stave ends, he swung
that hammer as if he stood on solid ground,
driving the wood on down. And thus it went,
we suppose, around and up, to thirty feet.
My father couldn't stand to watch for long.
That's all I ever heard about John Hummer—
who liked to push rare skills toward various brinks,
courting disaster with a kind of stolid gusto,
or grimly seeking ways to destroy himself—
except for something one of the farmhands said
when my father finished telling about the silo:
"Yes *sah!* John Hummer could *cut* you with a rock."

The Dining Room at Springdale

WALTER M. W. SPLAWN, 1883–1963

The Springdale Country Inn is two driveways
down from mine, so I go by it often enough
that I need not think, each time I pass,
of all I saw there, or heard about. Through childhood
I was a regular guest in the dining room,
at the dark table with the umbrella-belled
Tiffany lamp looming just above it,
the dumbwaiter in the corner, a danger
and a mystery, the dark-finished sideboard opposite
double doors through which, from the hall, I could see
Granddaddy sitting at the head of the table,
his eyes often closed, and when open, not steady,
for it had been many years since he had seen
the last thing he saw, whatever that was.

He said once that in the course of his last operation,
during which, for some good reason, he was conscious,
he became aware of a bad moment—a sound, maybe,
of breath sharply indrawn toward the shape of a swearword,
or only a sag in the room's energy—when
everyone there came to know he would not see again.

Still, he kept at most of what he had mastered.
You can read for yourself in a life of Sam Rayburn
how before he was Speaker he persuaded Roosevelt
to appoint Dr. Splawn to the Interstate Commerce Commission.
He knew his freight lines, by God. I used to read to him,
long incomprehensible pages of economics,
or a draft of his own history of the University of Texas,
of which he had briefly been president.
He would pay me a little something per hour,
for I had come early to the ability to enunciate
what I did not understand. That skill still helps me get by.

In that somewhat under-illuminated room we gathered
several times a year for Sunday dinner, or an annual holiday,
when cooking and serving became the responsibility

of Joe Trammel, a Black man with a deficient leg.
He had had polio. He got along by making sure
the bad leg's knee locked straight before he touched down.
He swung it forward from the hip, and his lower leg,
striking the end of its arc from the knee, gave
a small extra hitch to his uneven but durable stride.

I do not remember not knowing him.

One afternoon in the garden, when I was about three,
I squatted down in the path of his hoeing,
and the blade made its eager way toward me,
lifting the soil and slicing off weeds,
and I screamed, and he laughed.
Years later, as a crew of us ate lunch
and told stories, he said that ghosts won't hurt you,
but they sure-God make you hurt yourself.

When he worked the dinners at Springdale
there would come, sometimes, moments I can almost reenter
of suspenseful silence so heavy I knew how it would feel
to crawl out from under it. I never could learn
what, dimly foreseen—by me only?—filled the room
with overwhelming expectation, as Joe Trammel
circled the table and extended a dish-bearing hand
into the space above each place setting.
As most of us do once in a while, Granddaddy
would pull away from the room around him
into brief reverie. Being blind, he had gotten
out of the habit of pretending to alert presence;
he might tilt his head, close his eyes, and snap
his jaw, and you knew that something not in the room
was going vigorously on in that capable head.
He rarely took as much as half a minute, then came back,
having missed, apparently, nothing at all.
One night a few years before I was born,
there assembled in that dining room several men,
mostly Texan, like Granddaddy, and mostly,
like him, occupied with matters in Washington.
Mr. Rayburn was there, maybe young Johnson,
and Vice President Garner—old Cactus Jack,

who lived almost to the end of his ninety-ninth year,
and got into a few books of quotations by doubting
that the office he held was worth a bucket of warm spit.

But there and then, a fine evening, fraught
with laughter and good talk, winding down
after dessert and liqueurs, two or three old boys
still trading wisecracks, and Granddaddy withdrew,
then emerged, and said, "I believe it's time
for my warm milk, Joe." Then thought of his guests.
"I beg your pardon. I take a glass of warm milk
at the end of the evening. Would anyone else care for one?"
Silence of unusual heft. "Mr. Garner?" "Shit, no!"
The dry Texas hills crackled in the voice and rang
like sand against the delicate stemware on the white cloth.
"It'll make me sick to watch you drink it!"

Reporting this to my father, Joe Trammel
reminded him that you ain't supposed to let on,
when you're serving, that you hear what gets said
to others than you. "Couldn't keep a straight face
to save my soul, Mr. Tom. I had to set down
that tray and come on away from there."

My grandfather had that place for thirty years,
maybe a little longer. It had been a girls' school,
and a makeshift Civil War hospital. Such
are the glories that decline, in these
enfeebled times, toward bed and breakfast.

John Nance Garner, at the end of his second term,
retired to his home in Uvalde, Texas,
and the rest of his long life stayed out of Washington.

A Little Respect

From the farm next door, long after midnight, there came
one day last year the bray of a jackass, an unholy sound
I had not heard for years; by now it is nearly as much
a part of the air around me as the sound of my breathing,
but that first note set me off, down the hill and across
the meadow and up the road, then one farm north,
where old Foster was still working when I was a boy.
He assembled for haying a crew young and old, Black and white,
in an era when some men might have sent separate
and possibly equal water cans to the field, but Foster
had one can, one dipper, with which each man took his turn,
swirling the last swallow, not taken, into a jeweled
arc as he passed the dipper on and let out a breath
through his cooled throat like a velvet shout, and turned to work.

Down toward the edge of the bottom, then back into the hill,
two thirds of the load on already, and the mules balked.
It is a term rarely used in connection with horses,
for instance, whose methods of subverting human wishes
might be called stopping, quitting, refusing, or pulling back.
They shift about, under duress, to avoid moving on.
Mules balk. They put all four hoofs in touch with a force
below the earth's surface, and enter into a state
of patient remoteness not unlike prayer, or trance;
their apparent indifference to shouts, jerks, and blows
can lead their oppressors to an unexamined belief
that what they are doing is no more cruel than beating a rug.

So with Foster and his men. As usual, they tired first,
stepped back to take breath and wipe brow, and the air
settled, in nearly-noon sunlight, toward perfect stillness,
a transparency dense enough to suspend a fleck of chaff
or the odd wisp of hay, drooping weightlessly from the load
like a fern in a glass paperweight. Decreasingly labored
the sound of their breathing, and abrupt the halted buzz
of a fly landing somewhere. On the off side, the slight creak
of a strap under strain.
                        A boy spoke. Just a kid, a ward

of the county, sent out to this farm to be learning to work.
"Let me try," he said, and these grown men looked down
on this half-grown Black boy, then back at the team,
whose roots in the field were perceptibly deepening.
"What the hell," one of the men said, "he can't do no worse
than we done." So Foster stepped toward him, held out the lines.
The boy took them, made them right in his hands, stood
just to the near side of the rear of the team, and spoke
to the blindered heads. "Come up there, Mr. Mule."

First stillness, then a calm, slow lean into the collars,
a hoof lifted, and another, and they walked off
up the windrow as if bound for their hearts' desire.
The boy glanced back as he walked with them, and grinned.
"Call em Mister. It help sometime to talk to mules that way."

Here Reynolds Is Laid

It can surprise you to come on a tombstone
bearing a recognized name, unless, of course,
you are looking for it. I wasn't. Just wandering
in and around an old churchyard high up
on the Blue Ridge, and wham! there it was.

I was eight when I entered third grade,
but this was back before social promotion
had taken deep hold, let alone grade inflation.
One of my classmates was twelve. A big,
dumb goon, most of us thought, including
Mrs. Pritchard, hair-triggered, squeamish,
and, as Reynolds discovered, quite helpless
against waves of out-loud disgust when he spoke
of snot, or of blisters oozing watery pus.
He invoked her desperate paroxysms
almost daily in that one-room brick schoolhouse
borrowed from the Quaker Meeting for the third grade
the year we overflowed the main building.
A coal stove heated it, and occasionally scorched
to uselessness the single wet mitten left
out of sight by the stovepipe to be forgotten,
almost inaudibly to fry, filling the room
with a scent of burnt wool, evaporating snow,
the slow decay we did not know included us,
and even, as Reynolds at last settled down
for a while, a faint whiff of powerless rage.

An Artist from Another Place

ARSHILE GORKY, 1904–1948

Of the places the stream flowed through, one kept the name.
In my childhood, the 1940s, Crooked Run Farm
was the domain of Commodore Magruder, who came here
from all over the world, I guess, and fell to farming
with an amateur gusto that fueled many an anecdote.
Every so often my father would take his phone call—
some question easy enough for a man who'd had practice.
Instructed, Magruder would sometimes feel foolish.
"I might not know much about farming," he'd say,
"but by God, I could bring a battleship up Crooked Run."

His daughter, Agnes, lived off north, in Connecticut,
and came down with her family for the summer.
Her husband was Arshile Gorky, who stood once
just inside the door of the children's bedroom
in my parents' house and looked, smiling, around
at the plaster walls that had been left unpapered
so my sister and I could use crayons on them. Just one
crayon past our doorsill, and that would be that,
but this side of it, we did whatever was within
the scope of our negligible skill, our small size.
This stranger, then, whose two daughters we were learning
to "have over," looked out from under dark eyebrows,
spoke through his mustache, his Armenian youth,
saying "Bot! This is what I try to do!"
                                        Later on—
that same day? that same summer?—out in the yard
by the sandbox, Gorky stood at his easel, staring
at a space between trees, while his wife said "crayons"
so it sounded almost like "crowns," and explained his work.

A man like that living in our sort of country
could hardly keep from drawing attention—tall,
a touch on the shaggy side, sometimes unshod,
striding around on hilltops and by streams with a bundle
of crayons and a big tablet, making drawings

that could now account for nearly three hundred entries
in a *catalogue raisonné.*

                    The end
is there to read about. Car wreck, partial
paralysis, weeks of walking around in Connecticut,
hanging a trial noose on this branch or that,
Agnes sending the little girls out to play with him,
knowing he wouldn't do it if they were there watching.
The work and the stories endure. One time
Jim Cole, native farmer of few words, strong opinions,
drove in to the farm, needing to take up something—
wandering livestock, probably—with the Commodore,
but found no one at home and was starting away
when Gorky came out of the barn where he worked
and, spying the critic he had just felt the need of,
seized Cole by the arm and escorted him into the studio.
There stood a big oil, maybe part of the Calendar series.
Whatever it was, Jim Cole failed to perceive in it
accurate depiction of anything he'd ever seen,
so stood there in silence until Gorky pressed him
for a response, then said, "Waal. Flashy, ain't it."
For that story's survival we have the artist to thank.

Every once in a while, then, at the Modern, or the Met,
his weird simultaneity of hard edge and soft form
draws me back to those days by the sandbox; once,
the baby Natasha sat in grass with a ball,
striped translucent yellow and opaque red,
so the red cast a shadow across her arm,
and her big sister Maro, three, looking straight
into me as she held the handle of my toy wagon,
said, "I am going to take this wagon far away. And—"
here her chin crumpled slightly, but she held
her tears and went on, "I'm never going to bring it
back to you." I didn't know what to say; I was four,
and didn't believe her. Off she went to the far edge
of the yard, where I can see her still, walking along
the fence by the driveway. Doubtless she brought
the wagon back; yet more than fifty years later,
I've never seen past that moment of brave, purposeful trudging.

A Brief Partnership

One afternoon I brought the bushhog out
to trim the ragged hill above the fork
that meanders down from the old Hatcher place,
where Foster worked his mules those years ago.
I made one cautious pass along the fence
where rotted posts and stray barbed wire lie deep
in burdock leaves and multiflora rose.
After that swath was open all the way
the old Farmall would handle second gear,
and I could drift a trifle in and out
of the tall growth on my left, and gradually
straighten some curves and round the corners off
to make the steering easier with each round.
Then in the fresh-cut section on my right,
first not there then just there, a drab red fox
that trotted beside me for at least an hour.
I wondered if he were rabid or otherwise
deprived of his inbred distrust of men,
but then supposed exhaust fumes masked my scent,
leaving him only this sudden higher power
that gloriously transformed his hunting ground.
The bushhog blades were set too high to hurt
the rodents that they brought into the light,
but what my labor furnished, he could catch.
I still suspect he wasn't at his best—
mange, if it wasn't rabies, slowed him down—
but he was quick when a field mouse darted out.
We worked together there that afternoon,
establishing a temporary order
that summer stays ready to overwhelm.
I looked away when I had to, and there came
at length the look back that found he wasn't there.

Vision at Woods' Edge

Just a glimpse, doubtless nowhere near accurate,
through train window into the New Jersey thicket
past which we plunged in our self-absorbed hurtling
out of countryside into the urban explosion,
a mere glimpse: Farmall tractor squat on flat tires,
maybe rusted in place, three-foot circular saw
blade and log table mounted in front, and there,
running almost halfway from the edge to the center,
a crack in the steel, its ragged progress stopped
at a hole drilled, no bigger around than a dime,
yet large enough, if I step closer and look through
with one eye, to open out until I can see
the hillside above Uncle Will Smith's, the autumn
coming on, the men gathered for a day in the woods.

You might find this hard to believe. Just listen.
Long hours and short money will pave a mean road.
They mounted that saw on the tractor and went
to the woodlot, set up in minutes, and worked
whole trees into firewood and mill logs,
two men at the saw hoisting crosscut limbs
to the bench and down onto the blade, a sharp whine
for each cut, the stove-lengths flung to one side.
At quitting time one day they noticed the crack
starting in from a notch between teeth, so took
the blade loose and brought it in to the shop.
There, next day in good light, laid it down
on the bed of the drill press and stopped the crack
with a hole right at the point where it ended.
Then back to the woods, reassembled the saw,
and proceeded as if nothing was wrong.

Stand now where Uncle Will's pasture was,
look around at the fresh crop of houses encroaching,
and imagine, without passing judgment,
what acquaintance with firewood they harbor.
Where farm women toiled, soccer moms pool their cars,
and the skin of a pork loin is clear plastic.

Off there at woods' edge, where the trees have come over
the old barbed-wire fence, see the dead tractor,
saw-table in place but the blade not all there,
a piece taken out of it like a generous slice
from a pie. Look briefly, but look: they say
that when that one section spun loose it halved
a man's head as if it had been a melon,
laid it open like an anatomy textbook.
The stillness around the machine was not yet
what it is now, even after one man stepped back
to the switch and cut off the engine.
Just an eyeblink later, the abandoned tractor,
not quite vanished into this untended border,
is lifting the saw in the prayerful attitude
of a mantis, rigid enough to stop looking alive.

A Trace of Old Road Work

There was a time this road was narrower,
the blind curve sharper. In due course the state
was moved by equal parts of fact and fear
to smooth the curve with drill and dynamite.

One drill bit sank too deep into the rock
to be withdrawn, so they left it behind,
a pointing finger raised as if to mock
this stone-exploding urge in humankind.

When honeysuckle clambered to reclaim
the fresh-cut bank, vines covered up the drill.
A monument to nothing with a name,
it stands where I can show it to you still.

Summer Hill

"Seems like to me it ought to be Winter Hill.
Anybody'd stay here all year long listening
to the wind at night, that's what they'd call it."
Thus Paris Clark, of whom more anon. All through
the school year when we lived at Sycamore Bend
we passed by the place on the knoll to the left
about halfway home from walking up Ward Hill
from the bus. Clark came from somewhere else,
moved here when I was maybe eight or nine.
Before that, Florence Trammel had the place;
sometimes as we drove by we'd see her standing
between the house and the mailbox by the road,
still, Black, wiry as a storybook crone.
Her house was spooky: paint gone, set on that rise,
bristling with globed lightning rods, a ragged mutt
snarling around the yard, the old woman
leaning on her shoulder-high walking stick.
At last she died. A few months went by, and then
the mailbox changed, turned off-white, with big letters:
P G CLARK. We called him Mr. Clark; he did
day work when it suited him and my father.
He had some skills to a notable degree,
including anything you did with an ax
and some work that required a gun. He walked
with a limp, but I heard you had to be fit
to stay with him hunting anything up yonder
on Short Hill Mountain, whose woods he knew as well
as you and I know the way to the bathroom.
He looked as if he might have been part Indian,
as he claimed to be. My first glimpse of him
was at Coolbrook, where half a dozen farmhands
stood around my father while Grandpa and I
waited to one side. I saw the stranger there
ready to work, and asked Grandpa who he was.
"You don't know him? Why, he's your nearest neighbor."
Not long after, we sat in the living room
at Sycamore Bend while thunderstorms passed through,

and saw outside a figure in a bonnet
moving toward the porch. My mother let her in.
Spectacular, we thought, more like a crone
than Aunt Florence—yes, there's that Southern tag—
her eyes wide and shifting. Terrified of storms,
it turned out, so she sat there while they passed,
not speaking. I don't think she ever came back,
but later we got to dropping in on her.
Kimmie, Clark called her, and she herself
said her maiden name was Fairfax. She hated him
and was fond of saying so. She walked us past
pictures of her grown children, and a niece
either by blood or word, a young woman named
Arbutus Koontz. By one son, Cubby, she paused
every time we visited: a handsome, smart-
aleck-seeming boy with big arms. She told us
he'd been killed in North Africa. I forget
how long it was before I could understand
why she thought she didn't need to explain that,
but at first I thought he must have been some sort
of adventurer, and he may well have been.
I know now several things I didn't then,
and see more surely what she wanted us
to understand whenever she talked things over.
He beat her, I now believe, and otherwise
tortured her with infidelities.
These were local, involving a young woman
with whose father Clark had an arrangement,
believing you had to get it regularly
or lose the ability. I saw them once
walking up River Road toward the curve
where the spring was that he carried water from,
a young woman in short shorts, and Mr. Clark
with his hair slicked down, one arm around her waist.
Nearby her father sat smoking in his car.
And that was a realm, now that I think of it,
with which Clark had some unhappy history.
Cars, I mean. He got his leg hurt in one,
and ever after walked where he had to go.
Once in a while, if it was hot or raining,

he'd accept a ride, wedging himself deep down
into a corner of the seat and the door,
his right arm stiff, braced against the dash.
No use to tell him how little good that was.
He could handle an ax, though, as well as anyone.
He'd hold it in one hand and finish jobs
that others couldn't have started on with both.
He was using it when I first saw for myself
a physical fact that I'd just read about.
From the little rise part way out the lane,
I looked down to the hollow between our place
and his, where men were working on a fence.
Clark was notching a locust post for a brace.
The ax flashed in the sun, then struck the post,
and was back above his head before I heard
the blade bite wood. Sound can't keep up with light.

A Crosstown Breeze

A drift of wind
when August wheeled
brought back to mind
an alfalfa field

where green windrows
bleached down to hay
while storm clouds rose
and rolled our way.

With lighthearted strain
in our pastoral agon
we raced the rain
with baler and wagon,

driving each other
to hold the turn
out of the weather
and into the barn.

A nostalgic pause
claims we saved it all,
but I've known the loss
of the lifelong haul;

now gray concrete
and electric light
wear on my feet
and dull my sight.

So I keep asking,
as I stand here,
my cheek still basking
in that trick of air,

would I live that life
if I had the chance,
or is it enough
to have been there once?

II

My Dear Sister Hannah,

Carrie Taylor to Hannah Stabler
Our Distressed Home. Twelfth Month 3, 1864

It is clearer than ever now, we live
    in the land of rebeldom,
and we wait, after three shocking days,
    for what is yet to come.

We still have our roof above our heads,
    but every day have feared
we should not have it very long.
    Last Fourth Day night came word

that the Yankees were coming, burning up
    everything in their way.
We trembled, yet could not quite believe
    what we heard people say,

but next morning we heard it all again
    and then caught sight of smoke
rising from stock pens, barns and fields
    wherever we might look.

It was too true. They had come to burn
    all but the dwelling houses,
and a few of those were so close to barns
    as to be among the losses.

Smoke from haystacks in the fields
    was pouring up all around;
Uncle Bernard's and Mrs. Heaton's barns
    were burned right to the ground.

Such dreadful work was going on!
    We put the boys on guard
to let us know when they saw the troops,
    then Alice and I worked hard

at packing, for we were sure the house
     would go if they burned the barn.
Our nerves were stretched so tight we scarcely
     could guess which way to turn,

but at last we got our clothes together
     and more or less packed up,
then the soldiers passed by all around us
     and that day, did not stop.

It was said they had gone to Washington.
     We felt unsafe all the same,
and sure enough, next day, Sixth Day,
     about one o'clock, they came.

They rode up to the house by the dozen;
     our feelings were past description.
When at last we went out to talk to them
     they said they meant conscription

of all our horses, but we pled with them
     till they said they would leave one
besides the blind mare. Then they rode off,
     but another gang of them soon

swept down on us and took away
     the one horse that could see,
and set to driving off our stock
     despite all we could say—

the cows and sheep, even the calves.
     The burning party was stalled
a short way back, they said, and soon
     every corn-shock in the field

was hidden in thick smoke, from which
     small bursts of flame shot through.
One soldier rode round surveying the barn,
     to find which corner would do,

I suppose; we all went over to him,
    entirely forgetting our fear,
and begged him not to start the fire,
    and told him an officer

had already said they would burn no more,
    that we could keep our barn.
He said, "Ladies, I am an officer,
    and my orders are to burn."

William joined in the begging, too,
    but had so little hope
of its doing any good at all
    that he nearly gave it up,

but Alice and I got around him
    and begged, and almost cried,
as if we were begging for our lives.
    He asked to look inside,

then said, when he saw the flour kegs,
    "Ladies, it has to go."
Those words renewed our energy,
    and we implored as though

our hearts were near to breaking. Alice
    was brushing tears away.
Though I could not quite squeeze out tears,
    what all did we not say?

He looked irresolute for a while,
    as if he might have a heart,
then "I cannot burn it" said at last,
    rode a short way apart,

ordered his men to mount their horses,
    then led them from where they stood
all crowded around the kitchen door,
    hoping to rustle some food.

They took the saddle William had bought
        since the beginning of the war,
but oh, we were thankful they left the barn.
        Next day, another scare

came with the Yankees back down the pike
        just as a strong wind blew
straight from the barn toward the house.
        If the barn were burned, we knew

the house would surely go up with it;
        but they proved a small force
just riding by, not doing any mischief.
        William, without his horse,

had gone to herd up stock, while we
        prepared to leave the house,
the dry goods packed as best we could,
        the parlor carpet loose.

From us they took two dozen sheep,
        four cows—indeed, all our stock,
and I believe nearly half our corn
        burned standing in the shock.

They took our axe and butcher knives,
        even the carriage whip,
&c., &c. They left the barn,
        a miraculous escape,

yet we were broken as poor as poverty,
        and the whole neighborhood
is full of destruction. Everything
        that Uncle Bernard had

in his barn—wagon, implements
        of all kinds, his good sleigh—
all was burned up, and their house, too,
        did catch on fire, so they

carried most of the things out of it,
    but their servant girl climbed straight
to the garret window and threw water down
    on the roof and put it out.

They took Uncle Bernard's cows and sheep,
    even his watch. They are stripped.
Richard Henry's barn is gone, and Uncle
    Yardley's—although he kept

some nursery, so I hear—Tom Smith's,
    Will Smith's, out on the turn,
Sam Brown's, where Thomas Nichols lived,
    and nearly every barn

in this part of the country, most all
    the sheep and cows, complete
herds driven off, most of the horses,
    great quantities of the wheat,

corn and hay burned, Asa Janney's mill,
    and Watson's, where our wheat was.
Newton Taylor's mill is not burned yet.
    The only nearby house

to burn was Israel Young's. The worst
    destruction, we have found,
is among the unionists, but why
    has yet to be explained.

Second Day morning. I am ashamed
    to write so bad a letter,
but time is too scarce to write it over,
    and I might not do it better,

for the subject makes me so nervous
    I can hardly write.
Since I began this, another loss
    struck us Seventh Day night,

when our good blind mare died suddenly.
        William had ridden her
a day or two. She had the colic,
        he thinks. One thing is sure,

he has lost his last horse, poor man.
        He is down to one colt now.
One of our cows came home this morning—
        mine. Alice's pretty cow

is gone. Whole flocks and herds are loose
        along the mountain road,
and people are busily taking them up
        by stealth and force and fraud.

We have hogs, and would butcher tomorrow,
        but there is still the threat
of soldiers returning, for we have heard
        they are not done with us yet.

I despise the rebels more than ever
        for causing this awful mess.
Some weak-minded people will perhaps
        be more [*illegible*] after this,

but all I can say is they never had
        any unionism about them.
True, these were Sheridan's orders and men,
        though we could have done without them.

Alice thinks it would be nice to have
        a photograph of us
around the officer, pleading for the barn,
        but we looked so dolorous

I doubt we would gladly send it to you.
        William says ask Robert
if there is an old blind horse about
        he could trade for a bare cupboard.

I don't feel like starting over here,
    but if we went away
we would be beggars. Uncle Henry
    still has his barn today,

Uncle Aquilla's is not burned either,
    so close to the house they spared it,
and Jonah Hatcher's is not; he bought
    them off, as I have heard it.

I must close. How I wish to see thee!
    Alice has much to tell,
and would write, but is too near crazy.
    Do write us. Love to all.

                Sincerely thy sister.

III

After High Water

We park the car,
pick our way over washed-out stone
to the bridge, and stare
at what can be wrought in a single afternoon.

The air is wholly calm;
gnats drift unbuffeted between here where we stand
and the almost motionless surface film
above the minnows. Lift your hand:

the point it marks in the sunlight represents
the level floodwaters reached in less
than half a day. To left and right the rusty pasture fence
is bearded with muddy grass,

except where it is broken
by the passage of a tree, or most of one. Today
sun burns, flat grass unbends, and minnows betoken
the seeming return of all that was swept away.

A Straight Stretch on the Far Side
of Coolbrook

Henry S. Taylor, 1799–1866

From late childhood on, a fantasy I've kept
close to my chest is that I might meet old Henry S.,
at whose grave I've stood, in whose house often slept.
Neighboring Quakers made it their business,
when Coolbrook began to reveal what it would be,
to sit with him in inward inquiry whether less
of a house might better bespeak Friendly simplicity.
Who knows what that sober visitation wrought?
The rooms in silence hoard their deep posterity.

In the west gable date-stone, a year coarsely cut:
1827. Later descendants made
their own marks here, as postwar decades brought
fresh ways to pump household water upgrade,
or visions of a graceful first-floor bay window
at the front of the parlor, its foundation laid
in a hole dug at room's edge with shovel and hoe
by Edgar Brent, a Black man of kindly patience:
when my father, still in his high-chair, threw
his rattle so it landed by design or chance
in that pit at the parlor's brink, he would climb
out, toy in hand, and with minimal circumstance
place it on the high-chair tray. How much time
did Mr. Brent pass thus before I saw him myself,
gentle, distinguished, white-mustached, past prime,
dapper in straw Panama fresh from a clean shelf,
walking around Lincoln when I was just starting to?

I cast these lines back over the widening gulf
between now and then, when the farm was Henry B.'s, who
was the builder's grandson and grandfather to me.
I sat with him as he paged lovingly through
Henry S.'s day-book, teaching me to see
hints of the passions and tedium underlying life there
in decades before he had yet come to be.

Tucked in the book, a letter of late 1864
to a daughter away at school, about Union burning raids.
There are only copies now; the original is no more,
having failed to emerge from a senescent haze
in which my father unwittingly set it afloat
when he lent it to an enthusiast of local antiquities
whose mind was melting down, who simply forgot
he'd borrowed it, then died. We have the words,
the day-book bristles with that hand, smooth but taut,
and sometimes I almost believe, as I listen to birds
in old trees up the back meadow, that among them one
speaks for him. I turn toward the bridge whose last boards
barely cling to the beams, beyond it the road gone,
washed out, grown up in woods, so thoroughly effaced
that I can doubt it was ever there to drive on,
though I did that myself in a life long since past.

From here some thirty rods downstream, the branch
runs straight as a canal. The meadow lying west
of the bank is marked with faint hummock and trench,
left when the man made up his mind, somewhere
around 1840, to straighten that one stretch
of Crooked Run and shove it all over there
to the base of the far hill pasture. I glance back
at a picture on my wall, some years post-Daguerre,
small enough to cover with thumb, but no slack
in that tension of straight gaze, set lips, tight jaw.
A few hired men armed with shovel and pick,
a team of oxen, were all he required to draw
this landscape according to his will. At the end
of the Civil War he said he favored a law
that Secesh be deprived of the vote and bound
for life to the use of iron spoons. He was apt
to know what to think of my wish to shake his hand.

George Washington's Farewell to His Hounds

Some pillars of the Loudoun Hunt were gathered
to observe Tom Taylor's eighty-fifth birthday.
The weather on this last day of October
was warm enough to let us sit outside
where the sun was deepening its southward slant.
After a pause between stories trotted out

one after another, names of men and horses,
Joe Rogers recalled reading in the journals
of George Washington about the day his hounds
left Mount Vernon for good. He'd just about
hung up his tack; someone in Maryland
had bought the hounds, so he called them together

and rode up through the woods to the ferry
below Alexandria, put the pack aboard,
and sat astride his horse on the riverbank
while the hound-laden ferry pulled for the other shore.
Behind Joe Rogers's head, on the white brick wall,
a flake of paint had lifted, and it threw

a longer shadow in the steep sunlight
than you would expect from so small a thing.
It moved minutely upward while Joe Rogers
looked off toward the nearest hill and said,
"I can't help thinking he must have cast those hounds
a few times on his way up to the ferry.

Start one more fox." He kept himself from weeping.
"I wasn't there, but that's the way I see it."
A horse moved step by step along the hill,
nibbling the fading grass, and gave no thought
to history. The rest of us sat a while,
watching the evening drop a little deeper.

Brilliance

The first time I heard one adult call another a genius,
my father was speaking of a man whose face I don't recall.
All I have is the memory of an old Black man, climbing
with difficulty the few stairs to the porch of Janney's store.
A bush of gray hair billowed from under the back of his cap.
I can also see the front of his unpainted house, the worn stoop
and the door not quite straight, a few yards from the edge
of the road. The road has been moved in years since,
and the house made over.
                              I knew a little about what
the word "genius" meant; I was at the age
of comic books, and had begun to daydream
about the kid with the big head and thick glasses
who always had all the answers.
                              So what did he mean?

Well, Ed Harrington had come here from southwest Virginia,
the youthful employee of one Robert Gray,
called Colonel Bob, who bought the Glebe in the teens
and ran cattle there that he bought from all over the country.
They would be shipped to him on freight cars, arriving
just on the north side of the Potomac, at Brunswick,
or over in Winchester, across the Shenandoah. Colonel Gray
would drive his buggy to the depot, do paperwork
and take possession, and turn to this young Black man
and say, "All right, Ed. Bring em home." With the help
of a little old dog he actually called Spot, he would do it.

In that pause I was trying to think of a way
to make clear the incredible difficulty
with which you or I would have contended
with that simple command. These creatures
knew nothing of where they were. It might be
thirty-five miles by the roads Ed would take,
one man on foot with a small herd of cattle
who would see every lane opening along the road
as the way in to something they wanted. Somehow,
Ed knew what the cattle would think before

they'd had time to think it, and could take
some action.
God knows what.
But in two
or three days he'd arrive, the herd quite intact,
even calm, set free to rove over the Glebe,
the five hundred acres once deeded, in 1773,
to the Shelburne Parish of the Episcopal Church.
Its meadows embanked the North Fork of Goose Creek
a few hundred yards downstream from where
Crooked Run's water drops into it.

Colonel Bob
was a saddle-horse man, kept his horses to the flat,
bred and trained to show in five gaits—walk, trot,
canter, slow gait, and rack. He had the money
and knowledge to start with horses whose natural gifts
were abundant, but still, in that business,
brilliance is a matter of drawing out of the beast
an aura, a sense that the horse willingly restrains
coiled-spring energy enough to fly, or even explode,
as it steps high and quick, in sun-glare the metal
of bit, buckle, and stirrup agleam. Colonel Gray
had what it took, and he knew it. There was the time
he walked off with some championship or other,
and his nearest competitor, second to him all day,
said something sour about having the judge in your pocket,
and Colonel Gray stopped, turned, and stood before him
like a man about to fling down his glove and say
coldly, "My seconds will be attending upon you, sir."
But in fact said only, "If you doubt, sir,
that the judge knows his business, take my horse
into the ring, while I ride yours. For five hundred dollars,
sir, I'll beat you again." Nothing doing, of course;
the story ends there, or goes bad.

Ed Harrington,
meanwhile, squired over the vicinity the Colonel's
stud horse, Lincoln Chief, available for a reasonable fee
to impregnate local mares, and so in time came
himself to be known as Chief. And in time, too, tried

his skills elsewhere, left Gray's employ and went to work
for my great-uncle W. T. Smith, dairy farmer.
In the sphere of common farm labor, Ed was known
as a poor judge of the strength of materials.
In his care tug straps, trace chains, the handles of pitchforks,
to say nothing of more delicate mechanisms,
simply came apart, and gradually his labors
were chosen accordingly, though a colleague once said
that one day, having broken every piece of the harness
involved in dragging a log to the sawmill, Ed turned
in frustration and just up and busted that sawlog.
Yet Uncle Will managed to be pleased with his work,
and so a year passed, and one day Colonel Bob
came in the lane at a rack on his saddle horse, drew up,
and said, "Willie, Ed tells me he wants to come home."
"Well, Colonel, he's been a good hand, and I'll miss him,
but I don't see how I can stand in his way."
"Very well, and I thank you. He was all right, was he?"
"Oh, yes, just fine. Knows his cows, that's certain."
"Yes. Hm. Tell me this. Did he break up much stuff?"
"Oh, a little, at first. Here lately, I've had him at work
with a double-shovel plow. Not much damage to be done there."
In agreement Colonel Gray and Uncle Will laughed, but Tom Chinn,
who had stood by not speaking, now said, "Uh, Boss,
I reckon you better go round there and look at that plow."

One Way to Go About It

That little cottage not far from the school,
the story goes, once housed a smaller house.
A Sisk, they think it was, who lived there then,
woke up one day to how the walls drew in
too narrowly on his small but growing brood,
so took a notion to enlarge his place
yet keep on living in it while he worked.
He dug a trench for new foundation footings
just shy of a yard out from the old ones,
and came above ground level with cinderblocks.
From their private distances, the neighbors watched
how framing for new walls lifted beyond
the eaves-line of the house he was enclosing.
Sooner than you'd expect, siding was on,
the whole thing under standing-seam tin roof,
but door and windows were still no more than holes.
At last he was ready. The family trooped out
to bunk with relatives for a week or so,
while he went inside with a power saw
and a crowbar, and reduced the smaller house
to pieces he could pitch out through the windows.
They said it was peculiar, those few days,
the racket of destruction issuing forth
from behind such bright new walls and fresh backfill.
Plaster, lath, wrenched coils of pipe and wire
piled up around the base of the new house.
He hung the floor joists then, and covered them,
and studded out the rooms. The day arrived
when glass and painted wood closed up the holes
through which, all by himself, he'd thrown a house.
It might have taken longer than they say
when what they barely recall occurs to them—
a project rank with eccentricity
and magic, if not flat-out craziness.
But it happened, or they say it did, and I,
I think it over whenever I drive past,
and wonder what they know who live there now.

The Hayfork

I could get up from this kitchen table, I think,
and go see for myself whether, even now,
in the worn planks of the old barn floor,
there might still be two holes I saw made there
forty years ago, in a single second along
the ponderous time line of farming. Well,

I might get over there one of these days.
Meanwhile, what can I see from here? We entered
the barn's second story through a big sliding door
at the top of an earthen ramp. There was a haymow
on either side of a wagon-wide aisleway.
A rail hung from the ridgepole ran gable to gable.

High in a dark far end, when I was a boy,
the old hayfork still hung there, barely visible
in cobwebs and thin strips of sunlight
that burst between weathering boards. Shaped
like a three-foot inverted U, a giant staple,
it rusted toward absolute darkness against which

stark blobs left by last season's mud wasps
stood out like white spots on a heifer.
Who knew how long it had been there? Loose hay
was giving way to bales before I was born,
though here and there I've seen it made, the teams
of workhorses pulling the loader and wagon,

a man with a pitchfork working everyday magic
on top of the rack, the slow ride to the barn,
drawing the load up under the rail and the trip-stop.
A man dragged the fork down, hauling against
the tow-rope's weight the forty pounds of steel
with two barbed ends that grabbed the wads of hay.

Then the team, unhitched from the wagon, pulled
on the tow-rope, moving away from the barn,
lifting the hay toward the roof. A click
as the trolley-hook caught, then the hay

rode back along the rail into the mow
where men forked it away for the winter.

So to a day when I was twelve or thirteen,
when the baled hay we were making was plentiful,
stacked in the mow almost up to the roof,
and we were standing around in the aisle-way
after the wagon backed out, catching breath,
getting ready to go back to the field. One man

up in the mow took a notion and snatched
at the tag-end of rope still fastened to the hayfork,
so it whirred down the track to a place just above
the middle of the aisle-way, hit the trip, and dropped,
all faster, it seemed, than the noise of the track
could make us look up, and plunged its two points

into the floor just beside the left foot of Joe Trammel,
who stood there, leaning away from it, looking down
and then up, and around at all of us, a barnful
of men struck reverently silent in the presence
of whatever it was, the good luck that kept Joe
from injury, the bad luck that gave him his worst scare

in years, the innocent thoughtlessness that led
to that yank on the rope, the way things can go
for years without happening, biding their time
in a dust-whirling, cobwebby barn I can see
and smell and hear right now, staring down
at the grain in the wood of this kitchen table.

A Set of Hoofprints

A horse left this track as he walked.
Here a fore hoof made its print,
obscured as if by superscript
when hind came down where fore had been.
He turns toward home, extends his walk
till hind far overreaches fore
and every hoofprint is distinct.
You stand remembering how it felt
to sit those homeward-swinging strides,
to draw up by the darkening barn
and let your own feet touch the ground.

Valentine's Daffodils

I've stopped us here, my love,
upstream from Coolbrook, where the gravel road drops down
    between two hills that bear faint surface marks,
    the evidence of almost vanished lives.
        Just on the south side of the road
        locust and honeysuckle

        roil over man-made shapes,
all that there is of Richard Henry Taylor's foundry,
    where he cast farm bells, bullfrog-shaped doorstops,
    and a one-horse plow of his own design.
        Sometime in the 1870s
        he went broke, sold out,

        and moved to Delaware.
Across the road, beside this branch of Crooked Run,
    a cluster of shred-petalled daffodils
    comes bravely up each spring, out in that field.
        I don't know yet what they have to do
        with us, but there they are.

        In 1890 the land
belonged to my great-grandfather, who sold it then
    to William Valentine. The small log house
    was probably in place before that time.
        Though I have found several of them
        in my family tree,

        I'm no land surveyor;
still, one afternoon I drew a plat from the deed,
    came out here with the sketch, and paced it off.
    A rough idea, at least. On the west side
        a short two-sided spur stuck out,
        and where it ought to be

        I saw five walnut trees
I've passed for years without a glance, lined up along
    the northern edge of that small triangle.
    You know me well enough to understand

the way that sudden rightness struck,
then settled into me.

I stood at the back line
looking downhill toward the daffodils, then stepped
lightly over to where the house may have been,
sat down between two rows of new corn,
and tried to wake my nerves toward
feeling the very spot

where earth's energy spikes
out of a household's ashes deep under plowed ground.
Well. William Valentine—called Uncle Billy
in a weird southern likeness of respect—
died in 1918. I have stood
by his stone in the Black

graveyard. His heirs allowed
someone else to occupy the rickety cabin—
a squatter whose name just would not quite come back
to the minds of a couple of old men
who did recall, before they died,
the man's dramatic end.

This was some years after
he had littered the place with odd chunks of old iron,
the kind of scrap they would have melted down
across the road, if the foundry hadn't failed.
A sharp axhead amidst it cut,
one morning of snowfall,

the hoof of a loose horse
that crossed the road to the south hill, leaving a mile
of crimson tracks before it could be caught.
The man himself, whoever he might have been,
came one night in his two-horse rig
down past the Chappelle place,

the horses running away,
and didn't quite make the hard curve past the bridge.
Chances are it was the crash that killed him,
battering him as it did pretty thoroughly

into a tree. All the same,
       some people thought it odd

how cleanly his throat was slit,
and would not stop believing someone had cut him
    before the horses ran off, but nobody
    was able to say how. He was the last
       of the cabin's human occupants,
          though various animals

       soon came to shelter there,
and they included a mongrel chicken-eating dog
    whose owner's rifle shot had failed to kill him.
    He fled here, the owner close behind him, and turned
       in the cellar to flash two eyes
          between which the man tried

       putting a single bullet.
To spite hell the dog recovered, and moved on somewhere
    a little more hospitable and forgiving,
    but still clouds thoughts of the cabin with regret.
       In 1935 Valentine's heirs
          sold the place back to Taylors—

       my grandfather this time.
An aerial photograph taken two years later—
    probably as part of some New Deal project—
    shows the lopsided yard along the edge
       of the field; a dark patch within it
          may be the house, or only

       a charred spot on fresh earth
where the house had been. Either way, my father was there
    when they took down what they could, burned the rest,
    and worked things over with a bulldozer
       to give the place back to the field.
          That's what I know, sweetheart.

       We glance from that small rise
to the swale beside the flowers, guessing where the house
    could possibly have been. All that went on here,
    the wanting and having and going without,

the passion or contented calm
of every spoken word,

the pitiful belongings,
the names themselves: obliterated, all gone away,
and I feel now with the force of quick wings
booming out overhead from a low-hanging limb
that what I want is you safe from harm
and these flowers to hold us to that.

Aka Fawn Meadow

SPAM-2004-042 Application name: Hamilton Ridge aka Fawn Meadow. Project location: intersection of Sands Road (Route 709) with Taylor Road (Route 726). Request approval of Site Plan Amendment (SPAM) for a temporary sales trailer on lot 9.

Loudoun County land development applications accepted as of 5/29/04

At the county seat a map goes on display
to show the more than sixty lots these fields
have yielded to the husbandry of our day.
Until a wall of copper roofs unfolds

you might have time to catch a sunset's flare
beyond the trees along the old railroad—
not that there ever was a train through here.
Before the Civil War, bright prospects showed

a way to Harpers Ferry and beyond,
where West Virginia waited in its hills.
Though it bankrupted them, men shaped the ground
into a modest stretch of cuts and fills

that became a dump for agricultural scrap.
Now one of the streets carved on the stubbly fallow
is named for the railroad spur: Manassas Gap.
Alfalfa Court convenes across the hollow

to summon up the farm's last load of hay.
We find old words to call these new works by,
as if to name what goes could make it stay.
When mercury lamps wash out the Midnight Sky

and in Wooded Glen the bulldozed maples wilt,
settlers will ply the chemistry of the lawn
and high-priced rubber graze the fresh asphalt
beneath which lies the Meadow of the Fawn.

Boy Hunting in Bog

JOSEPH P. TAYLOR 1913–1926

Through a window before which I've sat
often enough to take it wherever I go,
I watch, down there in the boggy section
of the meadow across the lane,

no one I can actually see, as he stalks,
feet bare, pants rolled above knees,
in one hand a thin staff with which
he prods the mud just ahead of him,

hunting snapping turtles. That is the truth.
One crunch of its jaw could amputate
the largest of his toes, but he handles the probe
with a safecracker's patience and nerve.

This is a boy who once looked out
from a photograph hung on a wall
of his old room in my grandparents' house
and surprised me—I was eight—by looking like me.

Now I sit here watching, and listen again
to my father's voice, stilled forever, telling
how his younger brother grew deeply
into a world with wild animals in it.

What goes on is that the stick in its prodding
strikes a changed texture, and Joe—that is his name—
knows he's got one, and slows down, feeling
with the stick for the head, then the tail.

Though the turtle is deep in that muck,
the boy finds it. His hand plunges down,
then tugs slowly. The turtle hangs there, its head
like an erect penis, enraged, snapping air.

Did experiment teach him? He just knows,
as he knows where the orphaned fox waits
for his gentle ministrations, or the snake.
But deep in his own brain, something else

bided its time, and made itself understood
too late. It was 1926. He was thirteen.
When, as they said, God had taken him,
my father said God could go to Hell.

The picture hangs now in a room
set aside for stored things, not people,
and sometimes I go there to see it,
but mostly I sit at the window

through which I can conjure that meadow,
and watch as the bare-legged boy
grabbles in watery mud for a creature
to which all need is basic and sudden:

kill, eat, lay eggs, settle down
in black mud, and bring darkness
up to the light when it rises to air
in the grip of a child who has left me

forever between where his photograph hangs
and the bog where I still see him walking
with a heron's slow stride, pure attention,
not quite of this world, but deep in it.

On the Air

The lay of this field's land is as it was
when nothing brought word faster than a horse,
but the plowman in his closed-cab tractor has
equipment tuned to an ethereal force.
He hears the news and watches actual weather.
Today the candidates quarrel over a war
one of them may have started, though the other
could have it on his hands within the year.

He thinks of a dark night on a long driveway
when across the band of light before his car
flashed a tremendous owl, about a yard
above the ground, its great wings heaving hard
to lift a rabbit large as itself to air
or else to fail. It was gone before he could say.

Hughesville Nights

ὄρνυσθ᾽ οἳ καὶ τούτου ἀέθλου πειρήσεσθε.
Iliad 23.753

No one now alive, I think, was ever inside. The old store
collapsed into its own basement sometime around 1960,
having stood abandoned for close to a lifetime
there at the end of Bob Tiffany's driveway.
It was standing when I was in grade school;
I remember a low-hanging porch roof, a door
with an iron bar across it. All the wood
had gone gray, the paint disappeared, and the chimney
was starting to come apart at the top. Years later,
when I was living back there again, an indistinct heap
of crumpled roof and busted boards emerged
from thin spots in the briary overgrowth.
Locust trees grew from the cellar floor.

One thing that happened here, though,
probably in my grandfather's time, whenever
I think about it, makes me start putting the place back
together, making use of what materials I have.
                                              A small
general store, mostly staple goods and work clothes,
in the back room slabs of cured pork hanging.
On one side of the room a wood or coal stove
surrounded by objects that might once have been chairs,
or only aspire to be—nail kegs, say, or apple boxes.
Across the room, on the left as you come in the door,
the cash drawer and iron safe behind the counter
of laminated walnut strips, oil-stained, dented
and nicked. A low, weak place in the floor
where you stand to pay, or to have purchases
written down in the book.
                                    There are nights
after closing when men sit around for a spell,
a few loungers not quite done with the day.
A couple of oil lamps get turned up just a hair.
Squeak of corncob in crockery jug-neck,
soft boom of palm striking the stopper,

smoke in an undulant layer about even
with the tops of their heads. Somebody tells
another joke. Amid the laughter a notion takes shape
apparently in the air itself. Without a word
one of the men there reaches over and grabs an ear of corn,
shells off a good handful of kernels, and lays them
end to end, just touching, in a row perpendicular
to the counter's front edge. There is joshing
and nudging about who will go first, then
a cheer as one man steps to the counter,
unbuttons his fly, makes ready the implement,
and with it sweeps aside that part of the row
he can thus reach.
                By now the rest of the men
have arranged a rotation: each steps from the contest
into the committee of referees counting kernels
and calling out totals. Someone has the thought
to keep score on a slate, just a single initial
and a number. The row is rebuilt under watchful eyes.
One man sets a scale-weight down to mark a place,
another demands that two small kernels be thrown out.
The next man steps up, whips out and across,
takes the count. There are hoarse whoops
and high, loony giggles. "What color is that,
do you reckon?" "By God, you'd a got more
if you wadn't so crooked."
                  It ended somehow,
as such evenings do, in good humor or ill,
men stepping out into the night to sniff air
and make their various ways homeward over
the very hills and hollows I have lately been walking.
Among them there may have been a winner,
possibly more than one loser, but now,
however it was, there is nobody living
who could name a single one of them. The story
reached me as a curious example
of ingenuity in the use of shelled corn,
but soon enough the laughter dies down,
and it comes now to say that what matters most
about memory is what is forgotten forever.

Creek Walk

Strolling the banks of Crooked Run
I round a bend and happen on
a skeleton and rippling shreds
of bone-white skin in the oxbow pool.
It takes but a glance to identify
the stark remains of a tall foxhound
held in a nearly running posture
here at the end of a neighbor's pasture.
The open jaws might appear to say
we all must find our hard deathbeds,
but today I'm out to overrule
such hurts as I've been mastered by.
The earth's plain speech is all I've found:
no agony in the mouth stretched wide,
just water rinsing flesh away
and bones on their final seaward ride.